LAND
FOR BEGINNERS

HOW TO DESIGN THE PERFECT LANDSCAPE, WALKWAYS, PATIOS, AND WALLS QUICKLY: STEP-BY-STEP INSTRUCTIONS TO ENHANCE YOUR OUTDOOR SPACES WITH INEXPENSIVE IDEAS

Teddy Geis

Table of Contents

Introduction

A lot of people have dreams of having the most amazing front or back yard, an entertaining space to dazzle their friends, and be the life of the town, and the place to be for social get-togethers, but have absolutely no idea of where to begin. Most start with small-scale DIY projects such as flowers around the front porch, maybe a little mulch around the trees, or even a small raised garden with a few herbs (the legal kind, bring it back to reality, little dreamer). That is certainly sensible, but time-consuming. It could take years to get to the place that you have envisioned.

Some get somewhat of a design together based on what they see around them. These days, it's all about "Keeping up with the Joneses." Everyone is trying to have the latest and greatest to get the neighbors talking and get the adulation they so vehemently desire, so they immediately go into massive debt to get there. Whatever the case may be, landscapers and other contractors are raking it in.

Still, others are more methodical and get a game plan, save for each piece of the puzzle, and for a few years, end up with the "dream" entertaining space. This is usually the best option for everyone involved. Over the years, I've seen a ton of different scenarios from a full-blown paradise to what I can only describe as a "used car graveyard" to a hodgepodge of odds and ends scattered around the yard.

Whatever the case may be, whichever situation you are in or what category you may fall into, like any truly great story, start at the beginning and work your way to the final destination. Take the journey step by step, plan every little detail, and finally, DO YOUR RESEARCH! I cannot stress this enough. Whenever I go out to do an estimate, I always ask if they have had any other contractors scheduled as well. Sometimes, I end up losing a project because I'm not always the "cheapest" option, and I tell everyone that upfront. BUT I AM the best option because I will listen to the customer, get a thorough idea of what they want, and if I don't feel I'm the best fit for them, I will tell them. I believe in being honest and real with customers; it's all about them, not me.

The best place to start is to draw a map. Not a typical map but more of a timeline. Take a good long look at where your yard/entertaining space is now and put it at the beginning. Look at catalogs, the internet, local home improvement stores, etc. and find the elements you would like to have and add those. Make sure you're doing this on paper, a whiteboard, etc., so you can SEE the path. Believe it or not, this will help you make the best decisions and come to the ultimate conclusion.

Like any other major purchase, you need to have a game plan. You certainly wouldn't buy a house or a car sight-unseen, would you? I didn't think so. Therefore, you need to develop your timeline to make things smooth. Take pictures of elements you like, things you see while you're out and about, or save pictures you see online. Don't make impulse buys or fall for some "snake oil salesman" when it comes to improving your home. Your home is your castle; treat it as such.

Once you have a game plan together, and this is THE most important part, STICK TO IT!!! Do not get hit by "shiny object syndrome." Just because something may look awesome at the moment, it may not be right for what you're trying to accomplish. Take a picture, think about it overnight. Trust me, it will be there tomorrow. Once you find a decent, respectable landscape/hardscape contractor, they will listen to you, ask questions, and be able to show you a 3D rendering that should reflect everything you are trying to put together.

Locating Resources

There are several ways to locate the resources you need to create the space of your dreams. You have Google, a phone book, referrals, and several websites that contractors contact you after you fill out the form stating what you're looking for. Don't go with the first one that contacts you. Get at least 3 estimates for whatever the project is and weigh the options. Using the home and car example from above, you wouldn't buy a car from the first lot you go to, would you? I didn't think so.

Any home addition must be considered a major purchase as it affects your home's value. Think of the proverbial "Pebble in the Pond" effect. Before the tax assessment season, you decide to add a fire pit and benches in the backyard. The tax assessor notices this, and your property taxes go up by $300/year. It doesn't sound like much, but unless you're rolling in cash, it can be a major hit.

Now that you have compiled a list of contractors, take a couple of days to research each one. Look at both positive and negative reviews. Check them out on BBB.org and see what kind of rating they have and if they have any unresolved complaints. If everything checks out, compare them all and choose the best one. Remember, "You get what you pay for." I have to explain this a lot to potential customers when I go out to do estimates. I tell them all, "Yes, you can go with the cheaper option, and when that fails in 3-5 years, I'll be here."

Once you have the contractors, contact them. Explain your plans, and have them come out to give you an estimate. This will give you a solid projection of how much it's going to take to get your project done. Then you are one step closer to realizing your dream space.

As I said before, get at least 3 estimates for each project and compare them all. I cannot stress this enough. You never want to put all your eggs into one basket, ever! Now that you have your estimates, spend some time looking at the details. See what each one is going to include, and if any of them aren't exactly what you're looking for, contact them and ask them to amend the estimate to show exactly what you're asking for. Look at the timeline each one gives. How long is it going to take to complete the project? Do they show a breakdown of every element? Look at the charge for labor; this will tell you a lot about the contractor as well. For example, if two of them show a labor cost of $3,000, and the third shows $900, RED FLAG!!! More than likely, that contractor utilizes undocumented help, or they don't know what they're doing. Don't get me wrong, I have nothing against someone trying to make a living, but in my 13-plus years of construction experience, those situations never end well.

Something else to look at is "Equipment." The same rule applies; if one is completely different from the others, think about it first. Most, if not all, equipment rental companies charge about the same for their equipment. Even if the contractor has their equipment, they're still going to charge the same as if they were renting it. This helps them cover fuel, repairs, and normal wear and tear on the equipment.

One final note on looking at your estimates: Read the fine print at the bottom. I have several items in my contracts to cover my rear end when it comes to customers. These days, everyone wants something for nothing, so most, if not all contractors put in fine print different penalties for cancellations, changes, etc. If you have any questions, ASK. As I've been told many, many times, don't be afraid to ask. Remember, it's your money going out the door. Once all these steps are completed, you are then ready to move on to the next one.

Setting Your Budget

Setting your budget is one of the most important steps. However you decide to pay for this new venture, whether it be with credit cards, cash, or financing, you need to have a reasonable budget set aside for it. If I had a nickel for every time I asked a potential customer what their budget was so that I could work within it and still get them what they're looking for, I wouldn't have to work for a living. Make sure that you do your research when setting a budget. Do not expect Tiffany products at Wal-Mart prices. Remember, you get what you pay for, so if your budget is cheap, you're going to get cheap. There's a quote that I use a lot when talking to potential customers, "Good work is not cheap, and cheap work is not good." Let that sink in for a minute, I'll wait.

Figure out how much you want to add, where you want to add it, and go from there. If you know you can only afford to add a retaining wall for now, then budget as such. If you prefer to have the patio first, then plan accordingly. Never get in over your head. You don't want to go into massive debt to get the whole package now when you can prioritize, set the proper budget, and get what you want in stages. I've had customers start with a patio, come back a few months later, get a fire pit, benches, and a retaining wall, then a few months after that, a gorgeous water feature. Now, they're the envy of the neighborhood. All because they budgeted correctly, paid for it all with cash they saved up, and had a realistic plan.

When deciding on a budget, there are many factors to consider, but, again, you have to prioritize. Consider everything you want to have done, write it down, and go over the list. What do you have to have done first? What can wait until you save up some more? See where this is going? Put your list on paper, see it, visualize it, and go from there. It gives you a more tangible element to look at. When you can see your goals on paper, your thought process becomes a lot clearer than just going over it in your   head.

The Elements of Landscape Design

As a landscape designer for over 20 years, I have encountered a multitude of spaces in need of attention, whether they started off as a blank slate or became overgrown and neglected areas. The process of landscape design involves a series of steps that build upon one another, so I will start from the beginning with the basics. The more planning you do initially will lead to better results when your project is completed.

The first question I ask a client is, 'What would you like to achieve for this space?' One of my main goals is to create a landscape that is both functional and that will provide interest throughout all four seasons. Once the function of the space is determined, elements such as structure, form, color, foliage, and texture need to be taken into consideration when planning a space.

Function: When discussing function, consider the purpose you would like your landscape to serve. If you desire a quiet place, perhaps adding a small stone patio and a garden bench could create a peaceful retreat. If you're looking to attract wildlife, then the addition of a water feature, birdbath, or feeder could also be part of the thought process. Of course, function may be on a larger scale, such as the desire for a patio, deck, pool, or outdoor grilling and entertaining space. Once the function is determined, other factors are considered in the process of landscape design.

Unity and Balance: When designing, the different landscape elements should look like they belong together. Areas can be tied together by repeating elements such as form, color, and texture throughout the landscape. The use of similar groupings of plantings can help achieve this effect. It is also helpful to limit the number of different types of plants you are using so that the design doesn't become too 'busy.' Groupings of certain plants in odd numbers, such as groups of three, five, or seven, create a sense of flow and simple repetition, giving a stronger sense of unity. Odd numbers also allow for variations in height and are often perceived as a single unit that is not easily visually divided.

Balance can be achieved through symmetry. Symmetrical balance is achieved when the same objects (mirror images) are placed on either side of an axis, while asymmetrical balance is achieved by equal visual weight of non-equal amounts of form, color, or texture on either side of an axis. For example, while designing a front foundation planting, a grouping of flowering Spirea 'Magic Carpet' can be used on one side of a stoop, while a grouping of burgundy-colored 'Spilled Wine' Weigela can be used on the opposite side. In this case, the balance is asymmetrical with different foliage types and flowering times. In another example, a Hinoki Cypress with a grouping of daylilies repeated on each side of a front stoop would create an exact mirror image or symmetrical balance. The use of either symmetrical or asymmetrical balance will create the same effect of unity and flow in the landscape.

Form: The shape of an object as defined by a line is referred to as form in garden design. Form is probably one of the most important elements in designing a landscape. It is what is seen when first looking at a garden from a distance. Every plant has a distinct growth habit and shape that develops and changes over time as the plant matures. These shapes, whether upright, weeping, columnar, pyramidal, spreading, or round, define the spaces in the garden.

Pyramidal

Round

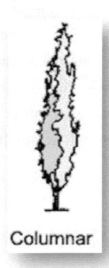

Columnar

Weeping

Broad

Oval

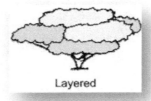

Layered

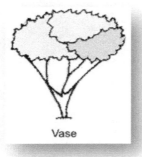

Vase

Shrubby

When describing the line of the bed, generally, straight lines depict a more formal setting, while curvilinear lines create a more informal look. It is best to maintain the same theme throughout the space to encourage uniformity. Also, be sure that the scaling, or size relationship between elements within a setting and its surrounding areas is appropriate. Taller trees can be used to soften and scale down a building, while smaller shrubs can be used along a foundation, such as under a window. When deciding on the type of bed outline or line of plant placement, I first look at the architecture of the home and any existing hardscape that is going to stay intact. If there are mostly straight lines, the design can be one of a more conservative style using straight beds with slight curves, or the placement of plants could be straight-lined rather than staggered. The opposite holds true if there are many curves in the architecture of the building or in any other factors of the hardscape. The use of curvilinear, or curved lines would then create more of an informal garden. The two styles can be combined if done carefully, but it is generally better to stick to one theme.

Color: Color plays an important role in garden design and is often more difficult to achieve in winter. It is best to plant perennials that complement one another (warm and cool hues) and those that have varying bloom times. For example, the deep purple blooms of 'May Night' Salvia (cool hue) are striking against the bright yellow blooms of Daylily 'Stella D'Oro' (warm hue). The bluish-lavender blooms of Nepeta 'Walker's Low' (cool hue) complement the delicate yellow blooms of Coreopsis

'Zagreb' (warm hue). For year-round color, add colorful evergreen shrubs such as Blue Globe Spruce, Gold Mop Cypress, Gold Lace Juniper, or Blue Star Juniper. For seasonal interest, add flowering shrubs that bloom at different intervals, such as spirea, weigela, azalea, rhododendron, orthosia, buddleia (butterfly bush), or syringa (lilac), to name a few. Take into consideration the fact that foliage and bloom colors of perennials and shrubs change with each season. The idea is to disperse color equally among the four seasons to keep the garden constantly looking at its best. It is also important to have a sense of unity and repetition to make the design 'flow.' Be sure to mass similar plantings for maximum color, and, as mentioned, combine colorful evergreens, deciduous shrubs, and perennials for all-season interest. It is also important to reuse the same plantings throughout the garden for maximum consistency.

Texture: There are three types of plant texture: fine, medium, and coarse. Plants with fine foliage have small, feathery, or narrow leaves, such as various types of ferns, sedges, grasses, or some varieties of Japanese maple. Plants exhibiting coarse texture display large, voluminous leaves, such as those of Hosta or elephant ears. In between are those plants with medium texture. Some plants that come to mind for exhibiting good texture, which I have incorporated into many of my designs, include Japanese Forest Grass (Hakonechloa macra), Hosta, Japanese Painted Fern, golden oriental sedge, ornamental grasses, Heuchera (Coral Bells), liriope, leucothoe, Weeping Japanese Maple, dwarf white pine, dwarf globe blue spruce, and weeping Norway spruce, just to mention a few.

Environmental Conditions - What to Plant Where: When selecting plants, there are several environmental factors to consider, such as lighting and soil requirements, cold hardiness, the size of a mature plant, and insect resistance. There are basically three main lighting requirements for plants: those that grow best in shade, those that require full sun, and those that need something in between. A shade garden is an area receiving filtered light with less than three hours of direct sunlight each day. The term 'full sun' refers to plants needing at least six hours of sunlight per day, but some plants, such as vegetables, require upwards of eight to ten hours of sunlight daily.

When discussing soil types, there are numerous scenarios. Clay soils, which appear as orange-tinged in hue, tend to retain much moisture and do not drain freely. Sandy soils, usually light in color and sometimes rocky, are the opposite, allowing moisture to pass right through, while loamy soils are rich in organic matter and hold water in moderation. Many plants do not fare well sitting in water retained by heavy clay soil, while others thrive in wet conditions. Some plants prefer well-drained soil, or soil containing a significant percentage of sand, where water will not accumulate. The best combination is a mixture of all three soil types. Along with soil composition, pH is also important, as many plants prefer slightly acidic soil (such as rhododendron and azalea) versus plants that may thrive best in a more neutral or even basic soil. Overall, it is important to carefully note the preferred soil conditions for your plants before planting and plan accordingly for the best success.

When it comes to cold hardiness, specific zone maps have been developed to categorize climates based on the lowest minimum temperature and the highest maximum temperature. Always try to choose plants that fall somewhere in the middle of the range for your zone. For example, if your location is in zone 7, plant varieties that are hardy in zones 4-8 should be used to ensure survival. If your area happens to get a severely cold winter with sustained temperatures near the zero-degree mark, it could mimic a much colder climate, causing plants to go into distress. The opposite is true with hotter than normal conditions. If the plant you purchase is hardy in zones 4-8, there will be a much better chance of your plant thriving should your area experience any adverse conditions. Choosing plants that are hardy in zones slightly warmer and cooler than the one you are in will alleviate any issues with survival.

There are several factors to take into consideration when planning your space. Following these basic design principles, along with the information to follow, will assist you in creating a welcoming and functional outdoor environment.

Vegetables as Perennials

Although only a handful of vegetables grow as perennials, there are many reasons you should include some of them in your vegetable garden. Not only do they come back year after year with minimal maintenance, but they are often virtually indestructible and can serve as beautiful, yet edible landscaping for your property.

There are seemingly endless benefits to including perennial vegetables in your garden. In addition to providing beautiful landscaping, they can help prevent soil erosion. Some perennials produce their own fertilizer. Many introduce nutrients into the soil that are needed by other plants. They can attract beneficial insects, and taller plants can provide shade for sun-sensitive varieties.

Of course, there are a few disadvantages to perennial vegetables. Many are slow-growing, so it can take a couple of years to become established enough to produce anything you can eat. Some perennial vegetables have strong flavors that are unfamiliar to American gardeners. Some must be harvested early to prevent them from tasting bitter, and while most perennials are low maintenance, if you ignore them entirely, some can become quite invasive.

This may sound obvious, but perennials take a little more planning than annuals. Once you pick a spot for these plants, they will continue to grow there year after year, so it makes sense to have a general idea of where you want them to reside on your property.

Here are some perennial vegetables, along with what you need to know about planting and living with them.

1. Asparagus

Asparagus is a hardy, cool-season vegetable that, unlike most vegetable plants, comes back every year. Its tall, vertical growth can be strikingly beautiful as well as delicious to eat. Although asparagus is moderately difficult to grow, the results are well worth it!

The asparagus plant reaches five to nine feet in height. It will spread from two to three feet wide and grows well in USDA hardiness zones two through eight.

The ideal germination temperature for seeds is between 70 and 77 degrees Fahrenheit. Asparagus prefers full sun exposure with a little shade. It is best to plant asparagus in acidic and dry soil that is well-drained and generously mixed with organic matter.

The ideal soil pH is 7.0, but asparagus will tolerate wide variation.

Asparagus needs well-drained soil that is on the dry side and prefers morning sun with afternoon shade. It spreads, so plant this vegetable by itself at the edge of the garden or in its own separate plot so that it will not disturb the growth of other plants.

Plant asparagus crowns four to six weeks after the last frost. Dig an eight-inch-wide trench and set the roots into the trench, one to two inches deep before covering with a layer of soil. Place each crown three to four feet apart. As the shoots begin to emerge, cover them with additional soil until you've reached the surface level. Water asparagus well, but not too much. The crowns will rot with too much moisture. By the middle of summer, apply organic matter and mulch to help the soil retain moisture. Remove any weeds that sprout up through the feathery growth. Prevent beetle infestations by handpicking or spraying with a hard stream of water to knock them off. Should plants become infected with crown rot or wilt, remove the dead leaves. Do not include these leaves in your compost pile.

2. Dandelion

You may think this is an odd plant to put in the garden when you are usually trying to get rid of them in your yard. Dandelion leaves are often used in salads, and even the flower, when it is yellow, is edible. They are full of vitamin A, B, C, D, iron, potassium, and zinc. As you might imagine, dandelions are virtually indestructible. They grow in any type of soil, any climate, and are incredibly drought-tolerant. Make sure to pick off the yellow flowers before they turn to seed, or you will have more dandelions than you ever wanted, spreading out everywhere.

3. Egyptian Onion

Egyptian onions are a rather strange vegetable, also known as walking onions. This plant is a self-propagating perennial that can serve as an interesting focal point in your yard. The vegetable is also delicious.

Egyptian onions are cool-season vegetables with a strong flavor similar to, but much more potent than, shallots. The plants are easy to cultivate and are very low maintenance. They are also called walking onions because they have the ability to relocate around your garden, replanting themselves. Consequently, you'll want to plant them in their own area, away from other vegetables. The plants grow to about two or three feet in height and spread up to two feet wide. They can easily survive frost and grow best in zones five to nine.

Egyptian onions prefer full sun exposure with a little shade. They grow best in well-drained soil mixed with organic matter and consistent moisture. You should aim for a soil pH of 6.2 to 6.8. Egyptian onions are grown from miniature bulblets. Plant them one inch deep into the soil and one foot apart, then just watch them go to town. After two years, divide the plants to give space for healthy further growth. The only pests that Egyptian onions are susceptible to are slugs, but these can be removed manually or by setting traps.

4. Garlic

Garlic is not officially a perennial, but it is treated as such in temperate regions. Garlic is a cool-season plant; it's an easily grown member of the onion family. Garlic produces white bulbs and is very frost-tolerant. In addition to its position as a staple ingredient in the kitchen, garlic is a natural insect repellent. The plant is also used in various healing remedies.

The plant grows between one and two feet tall and up to one foot wide. It requires full sun and well-drained, loamy soil mixed with lots of organic matter. Garlic tolerates many types of soil, but it grows best in acidic soil with a pH of around 6.2 to 6.8.

If your region has harsh winters, you can plant garlic six to eight weeks before a hard frost. If you live in a warmer region, you can plant it sometime during February or March. Garlic grows well in raised beds. Do not plant it where you've grown onions or garlic in the past three years. I also recommend against planting store-bought garlic cloves because they may be susceptible to disease. You can easily order garlic bulbs online or purchase them at a gardening center.

When it comes time to plant the bulbs, break them up, keeping the papery husks intact. Plant the cloves two inches deep and four to six inches apart, with their tips oriented upward. Rows should be planted one to two feet apart. Mulch garlic heavily after planting and remove the mulch around the sprouts come spring. Garlic is generally not susceptible to pests, but it can become diseased, especially if over-soaked.

5. Globe Artichoke

Globe artichokes are cool-season vegetables and members of the thistle family. They blossom in mid-fall. The buds eventually grow into the artichokes we eat. When artichokes go

~ 30 ~

unharvested, they transform into furry purple flowers that can beautify any garden.

Artichokes are a bit difficult to grow and may be best suited for an advanced gardener, but if planted properly, the results can be astonishing. Globe artichokes can provide your garden with beautiful landscaping and delicious edibles for up to five years.

The plants grow up to six feet tall and spread out as far as four feet. In colder zones, it is suggested to plant them closer together to guard against early frost. They can tolerate frost, but heavy frost can damage their stalks. Globe artichokes grow best in warm zones but can survive mild winters with correct care. They grow between zones six and nine.

The ideal germination temperature for globe artichokes is 70 to 80 degrees Fahrenheit. The plants require at least six hours of full sunlight. They require well-drained soil amended with plenty of compost to a depth of at least 2 feet. The soil can be sandy or loamy. Aim for a soil pH between 6.5 and 8.0.

Globe artichokes are heavy feeders. They require a moist environment, helped by generous mulching. They can survive dry conditions but may not produce as many flowering buds. As long as you use mulch to retain moisture, you may get by with watering your globe artichokes less than once a week.

This plant requires plenty of space. Wait until a few weeks after the last frost before planting. Add five inches of compost to an eight-inch-deep trench. Dig the compost down about 12 inches into the garden. If you grow the plant from seeds, start them up to 12 weeks before the last frost; otherwise, start by using basal stem pieces with the roots attached. Keep the plants well-mulched to hold in the moisture and feed them liquid fertilizer once a month during the growing season.

Watch for aphids, slugs, and botrytis blight. Control aphids by washing off the plants with a stream of water every morning. For protection against slugs, use slug traps. If any part of the plant is damaged by botrytis blight, simply remove the diseased leaves and treat the healthier parts of the plant with fungicide.

6. Jerusalem Artichoke

Jerusalem artichokes, commonly referred to as sunchokes, are North American natives and part of the sunflower family. They grow underground using tubers that look like little potatoes. They can be grown almost anywhere in the US, but the plant grows best in the north.

Between mid to late summer, Jerusalem artichokes produce yellow, daisy-like flowers on their stalks and sweet, edible tubers underground. It is a bit easier to grow Jerusalem artichokes than globe artichokes, and they are quite a fascinating plant that can brighten up your garden and provide your household with an edible ingredient for your kitchen. However, they can become invasive if not carefully managed.

Jerusalem artichokes are tall plants, growing from six to 10 feet in height. Begin planting in early spring, using whole tubers or tuber pieces. To plant, set your starts in the row every two inches and cover them with three to five inches of soil. Your rows should be at least three feet apart. Planting too late in the season can lower your yield.

Jerusalem artichokes love sandy soil that is well-drained and full sun exposure. The soil should have an average pH of 7.0. You can place them to provide a little shade for shorter vegetables. Before planting, work a generous amount of compost into the soil. Once the plants begin to emerge and have grown at least 12 inches tall, mulch with organic matter to help retain soil moisture. Although the shade given off by the towering plant will reduce weed growth, it is still important to thoroughly weed anything that does crop up. Water your Jerusalem artichokes once a week. Gophers, slugs, and snails can be a problem. Keep gophers and other small mammals out by building a fence. Chicken wire is usually sufficient. As for slugs and snails, monitor the plants for these pests and manually pick them off or set sticky traps to catch them when you're not around.

Landscape Gardening Ideas and Tips

In recent times, home and outdoor exteriors have come to receive a lot of attention. Landscape ideas to make the garden better are one that most homeowners follow today. The home's looks aren't necessarily determined by its interiors. The furniture, the curtains, and the interiors do play an important role, but they cannot complete the look of the home by themselves. The home's exteriors and the way they are treated are what generates the first impression. Landscaping ideas are one which has become popular in recent times.

With several landscape magazines and the internet providing a world of landscaping information, you now have many choices about your garden landscape design. The internet offers plenty of knowledge with photographs of other people's landscape designs and the final performance of the project.

When one thought of landscaping, the first thing that came to mind a few years ago was the massive expense and the drain on the capital. With access to so much knowledge, the homeowner can now use his imagination and time and undertake the landscaping project on his own, without involving any professional.

A number of factors must be taken into consideration in the landscape design made. The plan has to be such that it makes the best possible use of the available resources. Natural elements such as sunlight, water, wind flow, must all be provided due importance to the terrain. For each garden, the landscape design is made taking into account the owner 's requirement, the natural elements, and a host of other factors. So, implementing a landscape design used by someone else as it is for your garden is neither realistic nor recommendable. Your garden has its own unique characteristics, and thus, the landscaping ideas put into action must be such that you can make the best use of the tools available to bring out the beauty of your garden. Create modifications that suit your unique needs.

Planning is the first step towards a good design project for the landscape. You need to know your particular needs and make a plan that will take care of everything. Having advice from a professional landscape architect would help to close all of the plan's gaps and make it one that would yield a great result.

Getting plants of different kinds and trees is a wonderful and cost-effective idea for a landscape that would enhance your garden 's beauty. It is important to carefully select the plants and trees so that they complement each other. It is a good choice for plants that do not need too much care. You could be mixing flowering plants and trees with those with dense leaves. A lawn and a water fountain are some of the good ideas for landscaping you might find for your garden. A professional landscape architect consultancy will help bring new ideas into your landscape design.

Landscape gardening is the art of turning a paradise into a property or a site. It helps a person build his or her own oasis and comfort zone. There are some rules that must be followed when planning your landscape:

- Balance: The environment has to be built according to the needs of the customers in a balanced way. Balancing the area with the appropriate number of trees or with suitable furniture would avoid space wastage and make good use of the available space.
- Proportion: The architecture should be proportionate to make the region appear larger than anticipated; As in the case of a narrow property, for example, color or texture may be used to visually broaden the dimension.
- Focal point: The focal point shows the landscape's main focus that attracts the most attention. It can be like a tower, a sundial, or a fountain built by man. The focus

points make the eye travel the entire garden, which keeps the space exciting and gives a sense of calm.

- Simplicity: By not conflicting too many colors, textures, and masses, keeping it simple will bring out the design in a clear way.
- Protection: The landscaped garden, if the customer wishes, would provide security and privacy from the outside world. Some requirements might be regarding sunshades or special railings needed to protect your kids or pets.

There are diverse landscape gardening concepts on the market today. To get the desired look, various tools, such as color, texture, or shapes, are used. If you want the outdoors to be a part of the indoors, you can add a barbecue, patio furniture and deck to give your living room an extended look outside. If you're looking for ways to beautify your property, then it could be ideal to have a landscaping pond or to plan the landscape around your pool. A waterfall in a garden can make a fascinating addition to the landscape, no matter how big or small. A patio swing can be installed, too, to add a personal touch to your exterior. It takes preparation to make your garden. Factors such as the required color scheme, garden budget, and maintenance requirements must be calculated.

Landscape gardening can be done in a small way and on a large budget. The appearance of the front lawn can be modified by landscape gardening your driveway and made to look really appealing. It can be achieved by installing a fence or growing some grasses, or even using some trees because the front yard gives the house its first appearance. This way, you can add color, depth, and character to an appealing front lawn.

The selection of plants plays an important part in the design of your garden. Plants and colors, in a real way, bring life to your landscape. Plant selection depends on factors such as when they reach maturity, requirements for sunshine, tolerance to insects and diseases, and preference for soil. The selection can be made to make your vision come true in a very cost-effective way.

Landscape Gardening Tips

Landscape gardening has the potential to enhance the appearance of your garden in various ways. When landscaping your garden, tasks may include preventing topsoil erosion and weed control. Garden landscaping also provides numerous opportunities to improve the overall look and ambiance of your garden, ranging from basic garden design and layout to full-scale landscaping projects.

One of the easiest ways to achieve a specific landscaping effect is to use border edging in your landscaping projects. There are various border edging options to choose from, such as concrete, plastic, aluminum, tubing, and brick boundaries. You can opt for a single type or mix and match to enhance your garden's appeal.

It's essential to choose an edging design that complements the overall theme of your landscaping project, ensuring that it aligns with your desired look. If you lack the time to pursue your landscaping aspirations, numerous landscaping services are available for your convenience.

Meeting with the landscape gardener beforehand is advisable to ensure compatibility in terms of your landscaping project and shared goals. Many landscaping services are willing to listen to your landscaping ideas, recommend suitable designs and materials, and provide a quote that can turn your landscaping vision into a reality.

It's advisable to obtain quotes from several landscaping services before deciding which landscape designer to work with, as prices can vary considerably for the same job, and the quality of the finished work will depend on your choice. It's important to note that the most expensive quote may not necessarily guarantee the best results, and the cheapest option may have limitations.

Whenever possible, seek recommendations for a landscaper from family, friends, or colleagues, as word of mouth advertising often proves valuable. When it comes to landscaping your garden, the possibilities are endless; all you need to do is unleash your creativity, and your vision of a landscaped garden can soon become a reality.

Effective planning is crucial, especially if you intend to incorporate multiple features into your garden. Maximizing your available space is vital when landscaping your garden.

1. **Water Features**: Not all gardens can accommodate water features, but fountains and pools are popular choices. They can add beauty and attract wildlife.
2. **Trees**: Existing trees in your garden can be incorporated into your project. New trees can create wooded areas, enhance pathways, and provide shade for shade-loving plants.

3. **Footpaths/Paving**: Pathways can be paved or have a more natural look, using loose stones or wood shavings. Well-designed pathways can weave through trees and shrubs, creating an enchanting atmosphere.

4. **Ponds**: Ponds add charm to any garden and can attract wildlife.

5. **Rockeries**: Often used with ponds, rockeries offer a natural and rugged look and can elevate flat terrain.

6. **Seats/Benches**: Strategic placement of ornate wooden benches can serve practical and aesthetic purposes, contributing to a country cottage feel.

7. **Arches**: Arches and pathways create a secret garden atmosphere and serve as support for climbing plants like vibrant roses.

8. **Patios**: A patio area provides versatility for various functions in your garden.

9. **Gates**: Even without boundaries, gates or styles can separate different garden sections, each with its unique ambiance.

10. **Dining Areas/Barbeques**: Consider using one of your paved areas as a dining or barbeque space, allowing you to enjoy your garden while soaking up the sun!

Hardscapes

Remember, hardscape elements are hard features such as:

- Pools
- Ponds
- Patios & Decks
- Fences & Walls
- Pergolas & Arbors
- Outdoor Kitchens
- Outdoor Fireplaces
- Driveways
- Sidewalks & Paths
- Borders

Think about the hardscapes you want to install in your landscape.

Note: Plan the major items first - a pool, pond, deck, patio, pergola, terrace, fences. Then you can design your landscape around the large hardscape elements.

Here are some ideas for hardscape elements:

A. Decks

The decking or top boards for decks come in a standard 16 feet size.

When designing your deck, keep this in mind.

If you want a 12' wide deck, why not consider making it 16' wide if it's not too large for your design. By opting for a 16' width, you can avoid wasting money on cutting the decking lumber to fit a 12' width.

- On the same note, if you design a deck that is 30' wide, and your scale is okay at 32', go with 32' so you won't waste lumber/money.

- Find a free deck design tool online. Lowe's has a free online tool for designing your deck: http://lowestools.diyonline.com/servlet/GIB_Base/ lowes_entrypage.html?storeid=3002&from_entryp age=1

- IMPORTANT: You might need to obtain a permit to build a deck or patio. Check with your local building department before you get started.

B. Trellis and Fences

Add any trellises or fences to your sketch.

IDEAS

- A trellis or fence can be used to block a neighbor and provide privacy, but it can also give you an opportunity to add lines and color to your landscape design.

- Add another layer of texture and color to your fence or trellis with softscapes, such as shrubs, flowers, or climbing vines. Some of the best choices in the desert are Lady Banks roses. They're gorgeous and easy to train.

- Inexpensive Fence Ideas
- Corrugated Metal Roofing Panels - They're cheap. What? Metal roofing for a privacy fence? Absolutely. It doesn't matter if the materials are intended for use as a roof or anything else. Use your imagination. Here's a photo of a metal roof privacy fence.

Note: Lumber size is measured in depth, width, and length. For example, the 2 x 4 lumber you'll need for this fence project will be two inches deep, four inches wide, and whatever length (height) you desire for your fence.

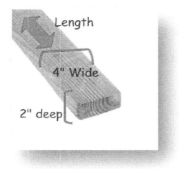

I love this fence because normally you'd use 4 x 4 posts for the vertical posts. But to save money, use pressure-treated 2 x 4's for each panel. When you attach one panel to another, it creates a 4 x 4.

Design your fence on paper first. Measure the length of your new fence and its height. Remember to transfer the measurements to your main sketch.

There are many fencing options, from split rail (country style), wooden pickets, wrought iron, cedar, or another type of wood plank, and more. You can soften the look of a fence easily by painting it and/or planting flowers or vines next to it.

C. Pergolas and Arbors

- Can you picture yourself sitting under a pergola, drinking iced tea, and reading a good book? You can buy kits and construct your own pergola for a lot less money than hiring a contractor.

- If you are considering a pergola or arbor, think about how you want to use it. You can find plans and kits online. A pergola or arbor is a great way to add shade to a sunny area and it can serve as an anchor to balance your   other   design   elements.

- Constructing a pergola or arbor creates a vertical hardscape element that will command the viewer's eye to take in the gorgeous structure from top to bottom. This focal feature will draw your eye to the top of the structure first, then down the columns to the ground. This vertical structure will make your space seem larger than it is.

- If you live in an area where the summers are hot, consider using an inexpensive misting system to stay cool. You can buy misting kits from your local hardware store and hook them up to a hose bib. It's easy, functional, and will keep you cool on a hot summer day.

D. Outdoor Kitchens

An outdoor kitchen is a fantastic way to enjoy the outdoors. Have you ever noticed that food tastes better when you eat outside? It's a perfect opportunity to incorporate lines, form, scale, color, and texture - all the basic elements! - into your landscape design.

If you're building an outdoor kitchen, keep in mind that you'll need power if you're installing a refrigerator, TV, sound system, ice maker, and plumbing if you're adding a sink or a dishwasher.

- Covered or uncovered?
- Propane or natural gas grill?
- Refrigerator?
- Seating area?
- Bar?
- Consider the location of your outdoor kitchen. If the grill faces west, it can be challenging for the cook during the late afternoon.
- Install your appliances just as you would in an indoor kitchen: for functionality. Place the dishwasher next to the sink and ensure there's plenty of counter space for food preparation, adjacent to the grill. You want to move around your outdoor kitchen with ease and efficiency.

- *If you're installing a cooktop, ensure that you have suitable ventilation located above the cooktop.
- You might want to consider purchasing a prefab kit. It's easy to install as a do-it-yourself project and is relatively inexpensive

The photo above features a prefab outdoor kitchen unit.

For a more detailed outdoor kitchen design, you can find websites that allow you to create your design for free.

E. Outdoor Fireplaces or Fire Pits

You can enhance your landscape with lines, form, scale, color, and texture by adding a fireplace or fire pit.

- Make the most of your yard year-round by installing an outdoor fireplace or fire pit.
- Choose a suitable location as it will serve as a focal point. Will it be on your deck or patio? Or perhaps you'd like to create a separate seating area elsewhere in your yard.

- Consider size and fire safety precautions, especially for overhead structures.
- Decide between wood-burning, propane, or natural gas options.
- You have the choice to purchase kits, construct it on your own, or hire a professional for the job.

- Will it be portable or fixed?
- If you're using propane or natural gas, remember that you'll need to run the gas line underground from the source to your fire pit or fireplace.

F. Driveways

If you are in a new home and the driveway hasn't been installed, or you want to redo your existing driveway, you have many options.

- Be sure to stay consistent with your overall theme (formal or informal, straight lines or curvy). You can use untreated concrete, stained and stamped concrete, pavers, or combine materials.

- Existing driveways (any concrete structure) can be rejuvenated with a straightforward concrete cleaning, etching, staining, or painting. Be sure to seal your finish to protect against weather and normal wear and tear.

- You can also enhance an old driveway (or patio) by adding a brick or paver edge on both sides of a plain concrete driveway.
- Staining concrete is straightforward!

To stain existing concrete:

- Begin by using an etching compound to make the concrete porous.
- Prepare the area by using plastic or drop cloths to cover the areas you don't want stained.
- Place concrete stain in a garden sprayer.

- Keep the sprayer in a 5-gallon bucket to prevent drips.
- Pump the sprayer and test it first on a piece of cardboard.
- Wear "booties" to cover your shoes.

- Spray the stain using circular motions.
- When I stain concrete, I can never get the color I like. I end up using three colors. I apply the darker color first and let it dry. Then I come back and spray a lighter color and let it dry. Finally, I mix the two colors for a third and final coat.
- It's the third layer of color that makes it outstanding!
- Be sure to seal your concrete after it has completely dried. Most sealant products recommend two coats. I use four coats and stay off it for several days because I don't want it to chip or scratch, and I want to avoid having to re-seal it anytime soon.

G. Sidewalks & Paths

- Take some time to sit outside and assess your yard before determining the placement of paths.
- Paths can significantly enhance existing features or new elements you plan to install.
- A sidewalk and/or path provide access from one point to another and can also help break up large areas, creating lines to achieve either a formal or informal look.

- Consider adding outdoor lighting or a border of flowers to soften the hardscape feature created by sidewalks and paths.
- Do you have a garden area in the back of the yard that can only be reached by walking across the grass? This is an ideal location for a path.
- What about a play structure, a bench, or a water fountain with no path leading to it?
- Is there a large, uninteresting area covered in grass or rocks that could benefit from a path?
- Think about a path from the backdoor to a sitting area or garden.
- Consider a winding path through the yard that leads to a bench or an arbor.
- Or maybe a path from the house to a patio situated in the middle of the yard.

- A path from the front door to the street.
- A path from the driveway to the front door.
- When it comes to selecting the path material, there are numerous options, including gravel, granite, stones, bricks, concrete, pavers, and more. You can even mix materials, as shown in the photo above, using concrete rectangle pavers and river rock.
- You can purchase concrete pavers in various sizes and colors. Before buying pavers, consider the cost of making your own by building a form and pouring the concrete.
- When determining the path's width, a general rule of thumb is to make it wide enough for two people to walk side by side, roughly about 4 feet wide.

Borders:

- Borders are typically installed when there's a transition in the landscape, such as going from grass to a flower bed.
- Decide where you want to install borders – perhaps along a flower bed next to the house, around trees, along the driveway, or alongside a sidewalk or path.

Types of Borders:

- One of the easiest and most cost-effective ways to create a border for your path is by making a shovel cut.
- It's FREE! To create a shovel cut border, use a square-edged shovel to dig down about 2-4 inches deep along the border or edges of your path.

You'll need to invest a bit more time in maintaining a path with a shovel cut border compared to using concrete, rubber borders, or curbing.

- Rubber Edging: Another cost-effective option for path creation is to utilize rubber edging. It's flexible, allowing you to create curved paths with ease.

Super easy to install. No digging is required, and you can effortlessly create curves. Take note of the flat edge where the nail goes in. You shouldn't encounter any issues mowing near the vertical lip on the rubber edge (no need for weed eating!).

Pick A Tool, But Pick the Right Tool

One of the best ways to save time in the garden is to use the right tool for the job. Trying to shape a hedge with hand clippers or loppers will take forever. Using shears or a power hedge trimmer will make quick, efficient work of the project.

With so many tools to choose from, the decision can be overwhelming. You might need a set of loppers, but do you choose bypass or anvil, short or long handles? The short answer is that probably any combination of the above choices will get the job done, although some combinations may be better suited to your needs than others. Consider how you want to use the tool and tailor your choice to that purpose.

Many tools out there are specific to one task, which could be accomplished with equal effectiveness by a more general-purpose tool you already have. A good example is a bulb planter. A bulb planter has a handle with an open-bottomed cone to remove a cone of dirt for planting bulbs.

Personally, I use either a trowel or a dandelion weeder, depending on the bulb's size. I dig down to the right depth, slide the bulb down along the tool to the bottom of the hole, pull out the tool, and replace any dirt. It's quick and easy, and I didn't need to own, store, and track down a special tool for the job.

For larger tools, you may need to consider whether you want a manual or powered version. If you only have a few small jobs for the tool, it may be hard to justify the expense of a power tool. On the other hand, if you simply want the job done as quickly as possible, regardless of the cost, the appropriate power tool may be the perfect solution. There are certainly jobs that justify power tools, which will pay for themselves quickly with time savings.

Hand Tools

1. The Tool Bucket

One of the most significant time-saving tricks I use is my trusty bucket filled with my most frequently used tools. I keep it on the back porch, ready to grab as I step outside. This bucket of tools will save you loads of time since you won't need to run back and forth to the shed or garage to retrieve a forgotten tool.

Actually, I have a pair of buckets that I use. The inner bucket is a small one, maybe two gallons, containing all my tools. This small bucket sits inside a larger bucket, which I use to collect clippings or weeds as I move through the garden. I slide a knee pad between the two buckets.

Once I'm in motion and have clippings in the large bucket, I carry a bucket in each hand. Since the outer bucket is large, I only need to empty it occasionally. If I only require the tool bucket, it's quick and easy to grab it and take only what I need for my current project.

So, you might be wondering, what tools are in my tool bucket? I always carry nippers, hand clippers, scissors, a trowel, short and long-handled pruners, and garden shears. I keep gardening gloves on top of the tools. In the scorching summer heat, a hat and towel join the gloves.

2. Gardening gloves

The first order of business is protecting your hands. Working in the dirt with bare hands can result in dry, cracked skin; the soil seems to suck the moisture right out of my skin. Scratches, punctures, and broken nails are also common byproducts of bare hands. A nice pair of gardening gloves is pretty much a necessity at my house. There are tasks where I need the dexterity of bare hands, but I wear my gloves as much as possible.

I use a washable pair of gloves with a nitrile coating on the palms and fingers. Washable is very important because, if you're anything like me, you'll occasionally get downright muddy. Then you wipe your face with your hand and... yuck. The nitrile coating semi-waterproofs and strengthens the fabric. I prefer gloves with fabric on the backs to allow my hands to breathe.

It's important to find a pair of gloves that fit your hands. It's nearly impossible to do intricate finger work with an extra inch of glove at the tip of each finger. It's wonderful that we live in a time where there are more sizes to choose from than just "large."

I bought a giant Costco pack of gloves about five years ago and am still using them. I'll break out my last pair this spring, and that's after sharing several pairs with friends. It's nice to have a spare set in reserve, so when your fingertip pokes through, you can simply discard the current set and grab a new pair.

3. Trowel

A good-quality trowel is a definite requirement. My trowel is my most-used tool, hands down. Don't go to the Dollar Store for this particular tool. Those cheap trowels will bend into a pretzel as soon as you put any significant pressure on the handle. You need something that is very sturdy, won't rust, and feels good in your hand.

My absolute favorite trowel is made of aluminum, which is very lightweight, washable, and rustproof. It has a thick, sturdy handle, probably at least an inch in diameter, that will not bend no matter how hard the dirt you are digging in is. The handle has a thick, rubbery coating to provide some cushioning and a solid grip.

4. Nippers and Clippers

The next two tools in my arsenal are nippers and clippers. They are my primary tools for deadheading, shaping plants, removing wayward branches, etc. I use them constantly, all summer long. Because they will get so much use, quality is strongly recommended. You want something that will perform year after year with little to no care. You aren't saving time if your tool breaks halfway through the job.

Nippers are for tiny branches, deadheading, and up-close, fine work. They have small pointed blades about 1" in length. Mine lock closed and have a comfy, rubberized grip. Keep them clean and don't try to cut too big a branch with them (my downfall, every time).

Clippers come in anvil and bypass versions. Choose what you prefer, as either will get the job done. I use bypass clippers that lock closed and have a nice ergonomic grip. Clippers are for cutting branches up to a quarter inch or so. A half-inch branch will be a real challenge, and you can hurt your hand trying to clip something that large.

You will notice that both my nippers and clippers lock closed. Locking them helps keep the blades sharp and also protects my fingers as I reach to grab a tool. Locking tools also have a smaller profile to fit into the tool bucket in a compact manner.

5. Dandelion Weedier

In case you are wondering, "What the heck is a dandelion weeder?" The answer is it is a straight, thin tool about 12" long with a pronged fork at one end and a handle at the other. It is wonderful for taking out weeds with long straight roots such as dandelions and buttonweed. I have lots of both of those weeds, so my weeder gets lots of use. Be sure to buy a sturdy one, as bendable ones are bound for the garbage in a hurry.

I use a trowel for killing weed seedlings, but as soon as weeds get a little size to them, my go-to tool is the dandelion weeder. It makes super quick work of loosening the soil around the root so that you can pull it or pry it out. This tool is also very helpful for bulb planting in the fall.

6. Scissors

Here is where I will advocate for using a cheap, disposable tool. I carry around a set of Dollar Store scissors in my kit. They are great for grabbing if you need to clip off chives or cut back a small, fluffy grass or fern.

Sometimes I will end up cutting something down in the soil, which is not so nice for my scissors' blades – rocks and such, you know. I also use mine to cut plant ties with a thin wire core, hence the preference for cheap scissors. When the blades get dull or chipped, I just toss them and go buy a new pair.

I do have a quality pair of garden scissors that can be taken apart for sharpening. They are sturdier than my one-dollar wonders, which comes in handy sometimes. I find myself gravitating to the cheaper pair of scissors whenever possible, as they are quick and easy to replace, and I can be a little careless with them.

7. Plastic Drinking Cup

Nope, the cup isn't for drinking. I use a cheap plastic drinking cup inside my tool bucket to corral all my small hand tools. The cup will hold the scissors, nippers, clippers, and other tiny tools upright so that they are easy to find and grab. No digging around in the bottom of the bucket to find those nippers, only to poke your finger on the tip in the process. Having tools that lock closed will make them small enough to easily fit into the cup with all their buddies.

8. Loppers

I carry two loppers in my tool bucket, both short and long-handled. They are the next step up from clippers in cutting strength. You can tackle branches from 1/4" to about 3/4" in diameter with these tools. Branches larger than that call for a saw of some sort. They are very helpful for fall cutback and for cleaning up and shaping shrubs.

You can easily get away with just a long-handled pair if you only want one. The short-handled pair is handy for getting into tight spaces but is not strictly necessary. You want something that can be sharpened if possible. My blades get dull and chipped with use. It is so nice to be able to refresh their edge every year or two.

Companion Planting for Vegetables, Fruits, and Flower Planting

Vegetables are some of the easiest and most rewarding plants to grow in your own garden. Companion planting in the vegetable garden can improve their growth, optimize space, and increase yield.

It's worth noting that members of the legume family (such as beans and peas) are valuable assets to the vegetable garden. They have deep roots that improve soil aeration for neighboring plants while extracting their own nutrients from deeper layers. Additionally, legumes can convert atmospheric nitrogen into a form usable by other plants.

Try planting your vegetables in groupings rather than ordered rows. This has been proven to confuse annoying insects visually, increasing your chances of some vegetables remaining unscathed. While one group may be repeatedly attacked, others may be left alone.

Consult the list below to find good companions for your choice of common vegetables:

Alfalfa: Alfalfa is a very effective soil breaker with deep roots. It's perennial, virtually pest-free, and can thrive with only natural rainfall. It accumulates minerals that improve various soil types.

Artichokes: Artichokes are a lovely addition to any vegetable garden and do well when planted with cucumbers. Keep artichokes away from potatoes.

Asparagus: Asparagus thrives when planted with carrots and tomatoes. Avoid planting it close to potatoes, onions, or garlic.

Beans and Legumes: Beans and other legumes enrich the soil with nitrogen when they die back, benefiting many other plants. They pair well with plants such as corn, brassicas (cauliflower, broccoli, and cabbage), beets, strawberries, cucumbers, potatoes, or celery. Avoid growing runner or pole beans with beets, as they can be detrimental to each other.

Beets: Beets enrich the soil with minerals and make good companions for lettuce, onions, cabbage, and broccoli. For improved beet flavor, grow them alongside garlic. Mint is also a good companion, although it may be invasive.

Carrots: Carrots pair well with many vegetables, including lettuce, radish, onions, and tomatoes. Leeks can help repel carrot fly, so plant them close to carrots. Note that tomatoes may stunt carrot growth, but it won't affect their flavor.

Celery: Celery is a beneficial companion to members of the cabbage family since its scent repels the white cabbage moth. It also pairs well with tomatoes, beans, onions, and leeks. In flower gardens, celery does well with snapdragons, daisies, and cosmos. Avoid planting celery with aster flowers or corn.

Corn: Corn draws a lot of nutrients from the soil, so plant it alongside beans to replenish nitrogen in the soil at the end of the season. Spreading plants like pumpkins or melons are also good companions for corn, helping to retain soil moisture. Other suitable companions for corn include potatoes, parsley, cucumber, squash, peas, or sunflowers. Pig's thistle is known for drawing nutrients up from the subsoil, making it a beneficial companion for corn.

Fennel: Fennel can negatively affect most garden plants and may kill many other species. Dill is one of the few plants that can survive in close proximity to fennel. While it can be invasive, fennel is an excellent flea repellent and attracts flying pollinators and ladybugs.

Horseradish: Horseradish is a good companion for potatoes, increasing their resistance to disease.

Lettuce: Lettuce thrives in the semi-shade of sunflowers and pairs well with vegetables like carrots, cucumbers, and beans. Avoid planting it near cabbage, as it can deter growth and impair flavor.

Onions: Onions are good companions for leeks, lettuce, beets, tomatoes, and strawberries. Chamomile can enhance the flavor of onions. When planted alongside strawberries, onions can help fight diseases.

Peas: As members of the legume family, peas are excellent for enriching the soil with nitrogen. They do well when planted with most common vegetables but should not be planted in close proximity to onions, late potatoes, chives, or grapes.

Potatoes: Potatoes pair well with corn, beans, brassicas, onions, and carrots. Marigolds and alyssum can benefit potatoes, with the latter providing living mulch. Avoid planting potatoes near tomatoes, as the two can contaminate each other with early and late blight.

Pumpkins: Pumpkins are great for baking, soups, and pies and can be stored for an extended period in a dark place after harvest. They pair well with squash, melons, or corn. Keep in mind that pumpkins require ample space to spread. Dill and oregano can provide general pest control in the garden.

Radishes: Radishes are hardworking plants that attract insects and bugs away from other vulnerable vegetables without damaging the radish roots. They deter rust flies, borers, cucumber beetles, leaf miners, and flea beetles. You can plant radishes among spinach, squash, melons, cucumbers, beans, and carrots.

Spinach: Spinach benefits from partial shade, making it a good companion for potatoes and bush beans. It pairs well with spreading plants such as squash. When planted with members of the brassica family, onions, strawberries, and peas, spinach thrives.

Sweet Potatoes: Sweet potatoes are good companions for root crops like parsnips. Planting summer savory can repel sweet potato weevils. Avoid planting them too close to other spreading plants, as they'll compete for space and sunlight. Sweet potatoes also grow well alongside aromatic herbs like dill and oregano.

Companions for Fruits

Picking fruit from your own garden is a very satisfying experience. Apples, stone fruits, berries, and melons are easily grown at home, loaded with goodness, and also make lovely gifts. By carefully choosing companion plants for your fruit bushes or trees, you will increase yield and deter insects.

Cucumber: Cucumbers thrive when planted with beans and corn. All three plants do well in the same conditions – full sun, plenty of water, and rich soil. Corn can provide a climbing frame for the cucumber. They also pair well with radishes, beets, carrots, and peas. Avoid planting them too close to potatoes and sage.

Grapes: Grapes benefit from many herbs like basil, hyssop, and chives. Planting grape vines beneath mulberry or elm trees has also proven to be beneficial.

Melons: Melons grow well in the company of corn, beans, and pumpkins. Oregano provides general pest control for melons, and marigolds deter various types of beetles. Nasturtiums also repel uninvited bugs and beetles.

Peaches: Peaches are susceptible to the peach tree borer. Garlic is a great asset for repelling these borers. When planted in close proximity to peaches, asparagus, grapes, or onions, they do well.

Raspberries: Raspberries greatly benefit from the close planting of garlic. Garlic stores sulfur and acts as a fungicide for raspberries. To repel the menacing harlequin beetle, interplant with turnips.

Strawberries: Strawberries are good companions for beans, lettuce, thyme, and spinach. Thyme, which makes a pretty border plant, repels harmful worms. Borage is known to increase disease and insect resistance.

Sweet Peppers: Sweet peppers are best planted in the company of tomatoes, carrots, parsley, onions, and petunias. Okra serves as a fantastic windbreak for these more delicate plants. Bell peppers make delightful ornamentals, so consider including them in your flower beds.

Tomatoes: Tomatoes are an all-time favorite and a 'must-have' in most home vegetable gardens. They have many companion plants: onions, mint, cucumbers, basil, beans, and marigold are just a few. Keep them away from potatoes, apricots, brassicas, and fennel. Planting tomatoes beneath walnut trees is not advisable, as walnut wilt attacks them. Also, avoid planting corn and tomatoes close together to prevent corn earworm infestations; separating them can help mitigate potential damage to both crops.

Companion Planting for Flowers

A flourishing flower garden is undoubtedly the desire of many avid gardeners. By thoughtfully implementing the principles of companion gardening, you can maximize the health and productivity of your flower garden. The results of careful planning will soon pay off, and your garden will be the envy of many.

Why not try the theory of 'decoy' plants? If you have a particularly pest-prone plant, try planting a similar-looking but hardier one alongside it – the shape and color of these decoy plants can visually confuse the unwanted pests. Nasturtiums are one of the most popular decoy plants. They seem to have a magnetic attraction to insects, drawing them away from plants that they would otherwise harm. Plants such as these are sometimes known as "martyr plants" because they suffer at the expense of others.

Many of the beneficial flowers that are good to include in your garden are easily grown from seed. Most garden stores sell seeds for marigolds, cosmos, and echinacea, all of whose flowers are irresistible to many pollinators.

The varieties listed below have unique companion properties that are good to keep in mind:

Chrysanthemums: Chrysanthemums are a perennial favorite, and some varieties are known to repel beetles. Costmary, a variety of Chrysanthemum, is known to deter moths.

Dahlias: Dahlias are a beautiful feature commonly planted in flower gardens. Their large flowers are delightful and repel nematode worms. Being taller and bushier plants, they can provide wind shelter for more fragile varieties.

Geraniums: Geraniums are perfect for repelling beetles and cabbage worms. Plant them freely around roses, tomatoes, and corn. They also help distract beet leafhoppers.

Gladiolus: Gladiolus is best kept away from cucumbers, melons, and clover.

Larkspurs: Larkspurs are beautiful, tall, spring-flowering annuals that provide a dazzling backdrop for low-growing hedges or borders. While they are a delightful addition to your garden, they also attract Japanese beetles, which die after consuming them.

Lavender: Lavender is an old English favorite and is renowned for both its beauty and fragrance. Lavender can be easily hedged, used as a backdrop, or simply placed among other plants for contrast. It is known to deter fleas and moths, and when planted under fruit trees, it will help repel codling moths. Because it is a prolific flowerer, it attracts bees and other pollinating insects that benefit neighboring plants.

Marigolds: Marigolds are perhaps one of the most commonly known pest deterrents; however, they must be one of the scented varieties to be of any assistance. They do keep the soil free of harmful nematodes, which makes them valuable assistants to many plant varieties. You can plant scented marigolds freely throughout your garden, keeping in mind that they do tend to attract slugs and spider mites.

Morning Glories: Morning glories are a fast-growing annual vine that attracts hoverflies.

How To Manage a Balcony Green

Having a balcony garden is a wonderful idea to brighten up your home, and it can make for a really enjoyable hobby. Managing a garden balcony can be a little bit tricky, so there are a few things you'll want to do to make it easy on yourself. If done right, your garden balcony will make a fantastic addition to your home!

Beginning the Garden Correctly

Check with your property manager to understand the rules for your building. Some buildings do not allow any plants (or anything else for that matter) stored on the balcony. It's also a nice courtesy to ask your neighbors if they are okay with you growing a balcony garden.

Not complying with these rules could result in receiving a fine or other penalties. Having your landlord or property manager on your side is essential, so this is really important.

Ensure any permission is in writing to have tangible evidence rather than just a verbal agreement.

Measure the area you have to work with. When measuring, consider that you probably don't want plants to cover your entire balcony, so plan conservatively for the space you have. You can use buckets or plates as indicators of how large a garden pot will be.

Ensure your balcony has a drainage system. Water-logging plants is one of the fastest ways to kill them, so you need to make sure your balcony drains properly.

Research what kind of plants you'll be able to grow in your climate. Some plants start small and grow to be very large, while others start large and don't grow at all. When buying plants, make sure you check with a store clerk or the information section to see how large the plant will grow and if your balcony can handle that size.

Buy climbing plants to maximize the space on your balcony, such as ivy, passionflower, or jasmine.

Consider planting vegetables in addition to regular plants. Many vegetables grow well in pots, making them ideal for growing on balconies. Some of the best vegetables to grow on balconies are tomatoes, lettuces, radishes, and beans.

Keeping Your Plants Healthy

Buy some gardening tools. If you've never had a garden before, you may not have the necessary tools to maintain it. They are very easy to find at any regular home improvement or home goods store. Some of these tools might be:

- Watering pot
- Pruning shears
- Garden fork and scoop

Make sure that you have enough time to maintain the garden. Unfortunately, balcony gardens aren't things that you can simply ignore and see flourish. They require about an hour of attention each week (depending on size) to make sure the plants are healthy, well-watered, and pruned. There's no point in creating a garden if you just don't have the time to devote to it.

If you live with anyone else, set up a schedule of various garden duties to help make it easier on yourself.

Arrange your plants so they receive enough sunlight. Plants have a variety of sunlight needs. Some require very little natural light, and others require large amounts. Depending on the types of plants you have, you may have to arrange the plants in a certain way to allow all plants to get their necessary light. A few of the plants you can grow in shady or no-light balconies include:

- Dracaena

- Bromeliads
- Maidenhair Fern

Opt for durable plants for a balcony garden. Founder of Plant Therapy Chai Saechao says: "In general, we don't encourage placing plants on a balcony. However, if you really want a balcony garden, look for cacti or succulents that will do well outside in the shade. Birds of paradise and yucca will also do well because they're very durable."

Dealing With Potential Risks

Place the plants in a secure location away from any ledges. When plants are located outside, they have to endure any weather conditions you experience, including wind. Many plants that are the right size for a balcony are also small enough to be blown over by a strong gust of wind.

If a plant is near a ledge and it gets blown over by the wind or some other force, there is a significant risk of it falling on anyone or anything below.

If you do happen to place your plants above solid ground in any way, they should be securely fastened and well supported.

Use organic sprays to help with pest control. Once your garden is flowering nicely, it's likely that you will encounter pests attempting to eat and destroy your plants. If you are dealing with caterpillars and other pests, using an organic salt spray, mineral oil, or garlic spray will help keep them at bay.

Many insects such as ladybugs, bees, and dragonflies are actually beneficial for your garden, so don't panic if you see them buzzing around.

Delay the arrival of winter with a bed sheet or another type of cover. Placing a bed sheet over your plants at the start of winter can extend the growth of flowers. However, winter will naturally bring an end to the growth of many plants.

You can leave root vegetables in the garden through the winter, as well as many perennial herbs such as sage and thyme.

Some plants, like geraniums, you will need to bring inside if you want growth to continue through the winter.

Do your research on how winter-hardy your plants are and prepare accordingly.

Tips for Starting a Balcony Garden

1. If you live in an apartment building or condo, does your building allow it? Be sure to check the rules for your building before you begin.

2. Can your balcony or rooftop support the added weight of pots filled with soil? Terra cotta and ceramic pots are heavy, so you might need to use resin pots, plastic or fiberglass containers, or fabric grow bags along with lightweight soil mixes.

3. How will you provide water to your plants? If you're growing on a rooftop, carrying jugs of water can be quite a task. You might want to consider drip irrigation or self-watering pots. Additionally, you can invest in a watering can that is easy to fill from the bathtub. Will excess water from your plants potentially drip onto neighbors below? Be courteous and place saucers or trays under your plants to collect any overflow.

4. What are the best plants to grow on a balcony or terrace? Choosing the right plants for your site is crucial. Don't waste space on something that won't thrive. The amount of sunlight is the most critical factor.

Does your balcony face south and receive direct sun all day long? Cacti, many flowers, and most vegetables—provided they are well-watered—will thrive there.

If your balcony faces north or is shaded by other buildings for most of the day, consider low-light plants like coleus, ferns, impatiens, hostas, and begonias.

Some greens like chard, spinach, or lettuce can grow with less than half a day of sun. Certain herbs also manage, which is great for culinary uses!

Many people overestimate the amount of sun they get. Keep in mind that most veggies need a minimum of 6 to 8 hours of sun a day!

5. Is your balcony or terrace windy? Be aware of any extreme conditions. The higher up you are, the more wind you are likely to have, and hot, drying winds can quickly parch your plants. Get double-duty from a lattice or wire trellis that can block prevailing winds while providing support for climbing vines, too. It will also add a touch of privacy. Since wind is drying, you really have to stay on top of watering. Look into self-watering pots.

6. Some of your houseplants might appreciate an outdoor summer vacation. Expose them gradually to their new location to avoid sun and windburn on the leaves.

7. How hot is your balcony or rooftop? Without the sun reflecting from windows, heat tends to be an issue. Lettuce would simply wilt. If heat is a concern, maybe go exotic with tropical plants! Just one pot of alocacia, banana, or canna can impart a jungle feel to the space. Succulents will thrive! Think of your balcony as a tiny outdoor room. If you have space, add a table and chairs and enjoy sitting among the greenery. If your location is too noisy, a bubbling fountain or some wind chimes may help add a bit of soothing sound to the background noise.

8. How big is your space? If it's small, we would suggest starting small. Yes, you can eventually think of vertical gardening, but a beginner should start with a few pots. You need to get a sense of how much time you have to garden and not overdo it. Arrange beds and larger containers around the outside edges to define the space and spread out the load. Make use of wall space to hang half-baskets and wall pockets.

9. Do you want to grow edibles? You probably won't be able to grow enough food to meet all your needs, but some pole beans, a pot of lettuce, cherry tomatoes, and a pepper plant or two will give you a fresh taste of summer.

Be sure they are located in your brightest spots. Learn more about container gardening with vegetables.

How to Choose and Maintain the Right Garden Landscaper

There are times when you will need to hire a professional garden landscaper to assist you with your project. This is essential, especially when working with a large garden or when construction work is required. In this chapter, you will learn about the factors to consider when hiring a landscaper.

- Qualities of a Good Garden Landscaper
- What to look for when looking for professional garden landscapers

If you are uncertain about how to proceed with landscaping, it's always better to enlist the services of a professional.

If you conduct an online search, you will come across numerous professional garden landscapers advertising their services. However, before rushing and hiring the first one who seems affordable or offers a compelling sales pitch, you need to consider several factors.

To make the right decision when looking for a garden landscaper, it's crucial to carry out adequate research first. Ensure that you have a clear idea of what you want for your garden landscape design. This will assist you in selecting the right landscaper.

First, establish your vision for your garden, or you might end up regretting your choice of landscaper. The landscaper might attempt to impose their vision on you. Even if you don't need to have a fully developed design concept, it's essential to have a general idea of what you want.

You also need to conduct background research on the landscapers before hiring them. This can be done by obtaining testimonials or references from clients who have used their services before. It's important to choose someone with a solid track record to ensure their competence and capabilities.

A good garden landscaper should have substantial experience. It's not advisable to entrust your project to a "rookie." Look for someone who has been in the business for several years and visit their premises. If their premises appear poorly maintained, it's a red flag. Ask the landscaper for references from previous projects and make it your responsibility to check them and view the projects to assess the standard of workmanship. Have direct conversations with the property owners and inquire if there were any issues. Was the project completed on time and within the budget? Were there any additional charges? Insurance is vital. Any professional working on your project should provide evidence of insurance coverage for both themselves and their workers before you approve their contract. Otherwise, you might be held liable in case of accidents or injuries. Ensure the landscaper is properly insured before hiring them.

Determine the type of garden landscape design you are looking for before selecting the landscaper. Different landscapers excel in various design styles. For instance, if you desire a formal garden landscape, choose a landscaper with experience in that specific style.

Define your budget for the project and obtain quotes from different garden landscapers to estimate the potential costs. Some landscapers may be more expensive due to their level of expertise or the companies they work for. Ensure you find a qualified professional who is also within your budget. When you draft the contract, include specific terms related to time, design, maximum cost, and include a penalty clause for any delays. This way, you'll have clarity on how much the project will cost you, and it will protect you from contractors attempting to extend the project to secure more money. Be aware that any changes you make after signing the contract could incur additional costs. A landscaper who refuses to sign a contract covering these elements may have ulterior motives. Finally, discuss the landscaper's availability and mutually agree on all contract terms to ensure both parties understand their responsibilities.

Make sure to establish a clear timeline for the project and discuss it with the landscaper. Confirm whether they can realistically complete the garden landscaping within this timeframe. It's important to provide them with a reasonable schedule to work with.

Arrange an in-person meeting with the garden landscaper before making your decision, even if your initial contact was online. This face-to-face meeting is essential for a detailed project discussion and sharing your vision. It also helps you assess your compatibility with the landscaper. If you establish a positive rapport during the meeting and effective communication is possible, it's a good sign that you can collaborate effectively.

If you have doubts about a garden landscaper, regardless of the quality of their references, it's advisable to continue your search for another professional.

How to Maintain Your Garden Landscape

Once you have successfully created your garden landscape, it's essential to learn how to maintain it and keep it looking its best at all times. In this chapter, you will discover some valuable maintenance tips.

- How to Maintain Your Garden Landscape

Effective maintenance is the key to ensuring that the landscape you've worked hard to design remains well-kept and continues to enhance the aesthetic value of your property over the long term. While some garden landscapes seem to mature and improve over time, others quickly deteriorate. The crucial distinction between these two groups of people lies in how they maintain their gardens.

1. Water

Ensuring proper watering is crucial to maintaining the health and growth of your garden landscape. Most gardens require regular watering. When planning your garden landscaping, it's essential to install an efficient underground watering system. Different areas of the garden may have varying water requirements, so consider designing the underground system to accommodate these needs. You may need multiple series of pipes to address the water demands of different plant types. Some plants thrive in dry conditions and require minimal water, while others need more water to thrive.

2. Fencing

The necessity for fencing in your garden depends on its location. If there are animals that could access your garden and potentially damage or eat your plants, a sturdy fence or a ha-ha should be installed. You might also consider a fence to keep your pets out of the garden.

In some cases, you may not require a full fence, but a well-defined boundary can suffice. Using rocks to create a boundary is an effective way to protect your garden landscape.

3. Mulch

For your plants to grow well and thrive, the soil must be fertile. You can either purchase mulch or create it at home. Regularly applying mulch around plants will contribute to the overall health of your garden.

Pathways and Entry Points

Access to your garden is essential for maintenance. You'll need designated pathways and entry points that allow you to move freely without damaging the plants or disrupting the soil. To effectively maintain your garden landscape, make sure to utilize these pathways when accessing the garden.

4. Pest Control

You may encounter pest issues from time to time. If you're not careful, these pests can attack your plants and potentially damage the garden landscape you've put so much effort into. You can address these pests through manual removal or by using pesticides. However, it's essential to stay vigilant to prevent this problem from escalating.

5. Wrapping up Plan

If you want to create a beautiful garden landscape, you should begin by making a plan. Make sure you have a clear vision for your garden landscape. You can conduct research to find inspiring ideas to incorporate into your design.

6. Vision and Reality

It's perfectly fine to dream and envision an incredible garden landscape, just like those you see in magazines. However, if you have a small garden, avoid choosing a plan that was intended for five acres.

7. Budget

It's also crucial to ensure that the plans you select fit your budget. Trying to create a garden landscape beyond your financial means is unrealistic and time-consuming. To help with your budgeting, visit online stores to research the prices of the items you need for your garden landscape.

8. Garden Style and Theme

Choose your garden's theme and stick to it while planning your garden landscape. For example, if you have a formal garden, ensure that your landscaping theme reflects this. This theme should guide your choices for all the items to be placed in the garden.

9. Ongoing Process

Achieving and maintaining a great garden landscape is an ongoing process. It's not a one-time task to be forgotten. You must take care of the garden consistently to keep it looking its best. To break the monotony and give your garden a fresh look, consider planting annual plants that you can change from season to season. Perennial plants last for at least two years, while shrubs can last for several years. Keep exploring new garden landscape ideas to help you refresh the garden's appearance and experiment with different designs periodically.

Is Edible Landscaping Right for You?

If you've never considered edible landscaping, now is the perfect time to start. But how can you determine if edible landscaping is the right choice for you? Here are several ways to do so:

1. **Love for Gardening**: Whether you're planting edible or non-edible plants, the essence of gardening remains the same. You dig, plant, water, and weed, making it a rewarding experience. Plus, many flowers traditionally considered inedible, such as daylilies, nasturtiums, and pansies, are not only safe but also healthy to eat.

2. **A Passion for Eating**: If you enjoy cooking and savoring delectable dishes, then edible landscaping is an excellent choice. Imagine having your favorite fruits and vegetables right outside your door—truly a food lover's paradise!

3. **Appreciation for Fresh Food**: Nothing beats the taste of homegrown produce at the peak of ripeness and flavor. With edible landscaping, you have full control over the quality of ingredients in your meals, free from mystery chemicals.

4. **Convenience:** Edible landscaping means you can step outside and pick fresh produce whenever you like, saving

you time and money spent at the grocery store. Enjoy more quality time with your loved ones.

5. **Adventurous Palate:** Edible plants come in a wide variety, ensuring you never run out of new fruits and vegetables to try. If you're not fond of the taste but the plant is visually appealing, you can always share the surplus. If you enjoy the flavor, then it's a win-win.

6. **Passion for Cooking**: Many top chefs swear by their kitchen gardens. For those looking to elevate their culinary skills, an edible landscape provides the freshest, perfectly ripe ingredients for creating delicious dishes.

7. **Aesthetic Pride**: Edible landscaping isn't just about growing food in your front yard; it's about creating an outdoor space you can be proud of. It's a way to make your home's exterior not only beautiful but also functional and sustainable.

Planting and Maintaining an Edible Landscape

Edible landscaping involves the use of aesthetically pleasing, food-producing plants in a well-designed garden, as opposed to the typical ornamental plants. While the traditional American lawn may offer visual appeal, it doesn't provide sustenance. An edible landscape offers affordability, fresh produce, a variety of blooming plants, ever-changing scenery, and a habitat for butterflies, birds, and bees. It can be designed in any style and seamlessly integrate both ornamental and edible plants.

This type of landscaping is often the least understood. Edible landscaping serves as an alternative to conventional landscapes that are solely focused on ornamental purposes. It incorporates shrubs and trees that yield fruit and various other types of food.

When it comes to an edible landscape, you have a wide variety of plants to choose from. Some of these options include chokeberry, almond, apple, bamboo, cherry, blueberry, currant, chestnut, gooseberry, loquat, lovage, medlar, grape, fig, dandelion, peach, pecan, plum, raisin tree, rose hips, rosemary, sage, strawberry, pineapple guava, and pistachio, among others.

While the idea of an edible landscape used to be inconceivable, these days it is flourishing in both cool and warm climates. It not only creates an attractive and beautiful landscape but also provides you with food from the plants it features. You can explore endless combinations, and even unusual fruit trees like persimmon, quince, and pawpaw can truly enhance the most stubborn and featureless landscapes.

Here are some principles to consider when creating an edible landscape:

1. **Diverse Variety**: Select a variety of crops with contrasting form, foliage, flowers, and colors.
2. **Layered Planting**: Plant in layers, providing a canopy for climbing plants, a middle layer for medium-height plants, and a ground-hugging layer below.
3. **Architectural Plants**: Incorporate architectural plants to make a strong visual impact in your landscape.

You can replace various aspects of traditional landscaping with edible plants. For instance, fruit trees can replace standard trees, perennial herbs can stand in for shrubs and ground covers, and they can be used for borders, flowers, and other decorative elements.

Mix edible plants with other non-edible plants to create beautiful combinations. Many edible plants can enhance the aesthetics of your flower garden, offering diverse looks and visual appeal. Nowadays, there's a wider selection of edible plants available, including newer and rare fruits and vegetables. This variety allows you to choose plants that are well-suited to your garden's location and your specific requirements.

Landscaping can be achieved in various ways, but the beauty it imparts is closely related to the selection and arrangement of plants. Typical combinations of plants involve the use of flowers, trees, and shrubs, all organized to create a harmonious theme that brings unity to all the elements within and outside your home.

Modern landscaping has captured the interest of numerous homeowners, but an increasing number of people are putting a modern twist on the most fundamental type of landscaping – the use of edible plants. This landscaping approach offers numerous advantages for homeowners. It not only enhances the appearance of homes but also elevates the flavor of your meals.

If you're considering this as a project, read through this article to discover more about the plants you can use and gain insights on how to maintain them effectively.

1. **Herbs**: Are you interested in organic meals without preservatives? Plant herbs in your backyard for an endless supply of flavorful food. Herbs are not only aromatic but also don't require much space to thrive. Even if you live in a condominium or apartments, you can cultivate a variety of herbs in containers.

2. **Vegetables**: Adding vegetables to your landscape brings color and vitality. Lettuce, eggplants, squash, and other vegetables can make a vibrant impact.

3. **Fruit Trees and Shrubs:** Dreaming of an Eden-like garden where you can pick fresh fruits in your own backyard? Plant fruit trees and shrubs. They not only provide beauty but also introduce different dimensions, layers, and shades to your outdoor space.

4. **Vines**: Many fruits and vegetables, such as squash, strawberries, grapes, and passion fruits, grow on vines. Vines have the unique ability to cover bare areas of your outdoor space, enhancing the overall look while offering shade and visual appeal.

Maintaining your edible plants can be as simple as understanding your plant species, choosing the right fertilizer, and ensuring a consistent water supply. Keep in mind that some plants may thrive in partial shade, so consider the sunlight exposure in your garden. Also, budget is a factor to consider, as creating a beautiful garden is an investment that includes ongoing maintenance costs. Lastly, commitment is crucial, especially if you intend to maintain your edible landscape organically. It requires effort to manage weeds and create organic fertilizers.

The previously mentioned plants are just a selection, and there are many other edible plants you can experiment with. Soil testing is essential to ensure your chosen plants can thrive in your specific conditions, as the health of your plants greatly impacts the success of your landscaping.

Hedges and fences can be valuable additions to an edible landscape. You can also use existing structures to grow raspberries, gooseberries, and currants along the fence. If you don't have a fence, consider planting a fruiting and living hedgerow. Rugosas are excellent for creating resilient barriers. High bush cranberries, blueberries, and raspberries are reliable choices that grow well in gardens. Always consider the unique needs and growth habits of each plant.

Edible landscaping not only adds an exciting dimension to gardening but also contributes to the well-being and health of your family. It's a satisfying experience to harvest your own food from your very own garden.

Designing on a Budget

While your budget will influence the type of patio you can have and the materials you can use, there are ways to achieve your desired look more affordably. During the design stage, it's crucial to avoid thinking too much about your budget. Overthinking budget constraints during the design process can hinder creative solutions.

So, what are your budget options?

As beautiful and durable as precision-cut and finished natural stone paving can be, there are more cost-effective materials available in the short term. Consider reclaimed paving, concrete, or basic natural stone as alternatives.

Another way to make your budget work for you is by phasing your project. If you have your heart set on LED lighting but your current budget doesn't allow for it, consider installing ducting pipes under the patio. This will allow you to feed an electric cable through at a later date when your budget permits it.

The same approach can be applied to raised planters and built-in seating. They don't have to be constructed simultaneously with the patio. A skilled contractor should be willing to break down the project into manageable phases, especially if they expect to secure future work.

However, certain tasks are more efficient when completed in one go. For example, bringing machinery on-site to excavate footings or perform clearance is cost-effective as a single operation. Additionally, you wouldn't want heavy machinery traversing your beautiful new patio at a later date.

Hiring a Contractor

When hiring a contractor, it's crucial to find someone you can trust. Request a quote for the complete garden project, and express your desire to tackle it in phases. Provide them with your budget and inquire about the options and services they can offer to align with your financial constraints.

A reputable contractor will not shortchange you by providing inadequate work within your budget. They will aim to maximize the value of your budget, understanding that satisfactory completion of phase one increases the likelihood of being rehired for subsequent phases. However, it's essential to acknowledge that untrustworthy contractors exist. Therefore, exercise caution, carefully select your contractor, request references, and review their past projects.

How to Determine if a Contractor is Likely to be Good or Not

There will always be exceptions to the rule, of course, but the good contractors tend to exhibit the following characteristics:

They take immense pride in their work and prioritize quality over rushing to meet fixed prices.

Their work tools are well-organized and maintained, even if not brand new, ensuring they are in impeccable condition.

Good contractors leave the work site clean and tidy daily, ensuring any dug holes are safely secured for the client.

If they cannot meet a start date, they communicate and reschedule promptly.

Additionally, reputable contractors typically work with a fixed price rather than providing estimates, which tend to be lower to secure the work. When hiring, be cautious about day rates, as they may lead to unexpected delays, as I personally experienced twice and have vowed never to do it again. Even someone I'd known since childhood, whom I trusted, took a week to complete a wall that should have taken a maximum of 2-3 days.

The unfortunate clients who had the misfortune of hiring bad contractors shared several common issues. These unreliable contractors exhibited the following traits:

1. They lacked punctuality and often showed up whenever they pleased.
2. They struggled to interpret plans correctly, often deviating from the intended design.
3. The interiors of their vehicles were disorganized, resembling trashcans, and their tools were haphazardly scattered in the back of their vans.

Keep in mind that the appearance of the contractor's vehicle, whether new or not, can offer insight into their professionalism. A tidy, organized interior often reflects a more conscientious mentality. However, a messy vehicle doesn't necessarily imply a lack of skill. It's crucial to evaluate other aspects of their workmanship. If you observe any of the aforementioned warning signs, it's advisable to find another contractor quickly.

Whenever possible, visit projects the contractor has completed for previous clients. While they can provide photos of their work, it's not a guarantee that the work is genuinely theirs.

Visual Clues to Consider When Assessing a Contractor's Work:

1. Ensure there are no puddles on the patio. Proper drainage should direct water away from the house. If that's not feasible, a drain should prevent water from collecting near walls or on the patio.

2. Pay close attention to any cut paving; it should have a clean edge and seamlessly integrate with surrounding paving. Damaged paving should not be used. Joints (the gaps between slabs) should be evenly spaced. While this may not always be achievable with older-style paving, it's still essential to watch for consistency. Check that joints form straight lines throughout the entire patio, without gradually veering off to one side.

In a good example of a patio, one crucial aspect to consider is the contractor's ability to create circular-shaped patios by hand (not using preformed circle kits). Focus on the curvature and assess how circular it appears. Some contractors may attempt a semi-circular design that resembles a hexagon. If any part of the circle appears straight, it's a clear sign that they may not be the right contractor for your project.

For a bad example, examine the curved edges (with red lines indicating the 'straight' sections of the circle). In the example on the right, the paving joints are uneven, and a portion of the slab corner has been broken off.

Materials

The choice of materials for constructing your patio will significantly impact its appearance, feel, and cost. You have various options, including reclaimed paving, concrete, natural stone, clay pavers, concrete pavers, and pressed concrete.

Which Paving Materials Should You Use? When selecting paving materials, consider the following factors:

1. Color, Texture, and Size
2. Garden Style
3. Property and Location
4. Price and Longevity
5. Environmental Impact

Color, Texture, and Size Color is often a crucial consideration when choosing your paving materials. Several factors should be taken into account. First, consider the color of your property. Examine your house and decide whether you want patio materials that contrast with or match it.

Another important aspect is the amount of light in the area. For instance, grey paving slabs may appear dull and gloomy in regions with limited sunlight. If you reside in the UK, this might sound familiar! However, dark grey or black paving, such as slate, can work well when the surrounding area is well-illuminated. For instance, a cream or white house in full sunlight can complement very dark paving.

Texture is another very important thing to consider. If parts of your patio are in shade, then choosing paving with a rougher texture is advisable as there will be more raised surface for your foot to grip. Natural stone and concrete can have what's called a riven surface, which is slightly rough and uneven. Try to avoid very riven paving if you are planning on having table and chairs on your patio, as the unevenness can make for wobbly furniture.

The size of the paving can also dramatically affect the look and feel of your patio. This is especially the case with small areas. In this case, if you use the smallest sizes of paving you can find, this will make the patio look and feel larger as the additional quantity of paving required will fool your eyes into assuming the area is large.

Garden Style

Choose a paving slab that works not only with what's in your home, but also the style of garden you are creating. Rustic, riven paving might look out of place with a very modern home and garden. The same goes for perfectly cut, smooth modern paving, which could look very odd in a country cottage garden.

NATURAL STONE PAVING WITH 'TUMBLED' EDGES, MAKES THE SLABS LOOK OLDER AND CREATES A TRADITIONAL LOOK AND FEEL.

MODERN, SMOOTH, NATURAL STONE PAVING IN LIGHT AND DARK COLOURS

Property and Location

If you have access to local natural stone, this is a good option as it's likely to harmonize naturally with your house and location. Natural stones are quarried from various regions worldwide, and while they are more aesthetically pleasing than concrete, not all types will complement your property.

Whether you opt for natural stone or concrete paving, it's advisable to bring home a selection from the builders' merchant to assess how they blend with your garden and house. Consider taking at least two or three samples of each type, as there may be some color variations. Examining multiple materials helps in making an informed decision. Even if you have to pay for samples, you can return the ones you decide against and request a refund.

Price and Longevity

Your budget will influence your choice of paving, but don't automatically assume that concrete paving is more cost-effective than natural stone. Natural stone offers better aesthetics and longevity. Concrete paving tends to deteriorate with time and doesn't clean as effectively as natural stone.

Another option is to go for a pressed concrete patio, which is created by adding a concrete colorant and pressing a pattern into it, resulting in a designed surface. This material holds up slightly better than standard concrete paving slabs, but it can still develop cracks, and its color may fade over time.

Environmental Impact

The environmental impact of patio materials is a complex issue due to limited ideal solutions. Both concrete and natural stone paving have significant environmental impacts. Concrete is notably harmful, while natural stone often requires long-distance shipping, primarily from India, China, and Turkey.

The natural stone industry sometimes involves child labor and falls short in safety standards. Responsible companies do ensure adherence to proper health and safety laws and worker age requirements, but child labor persists in some cases.

If you prefer to use natural stone, which is the more environmentally friendly choice and offers longer durability compared to concrete, consider buying locally sourced stone if it fits your budget. Although it may be more expensive than Indian sandstone, it results in less human and environmental impact.

Another option is to opt for reclaimed stone. While this can also be relatively costly, it's an excellent choice for achieving a well-worn, vintage appearance.

Conclusion

Whatever the project may be, whether it's a large-scale endeavor or a simple landscaping task, design is the most crucial aspect to consider in order to formulate a plan and subsequently take action.

Residential Landscaping

In any undertaking we choose in life, there are aspects to contemplate before devising a plan. The same holds true if you wish to renovate your lawn, as there are factors to examine and ideas to consider before commencing the process.

Why Do You Want to Do It?

If the idea is to give your yard some form of renovation through landscaping, then the possibilities regarding what you'd like the outcome to be are endless. You can call the shots according to your current preferences when you want it done. On the other hand, if you decide to sell the property, you must give the landscaping design a more sophisticated look. This is also a way to be safe, as not every potential buyer would want an unfamiliar style. With something simple and classy, you could never go wrong. It would also be to your advantage because it will add more value to what you're selling, and more people will be enticed to look at it and consider a deal.

What Do You Want to Be Done?

For people who'd like to do their landscaping, the American Nursery and Landscape Association (ANLA) says that it is important for the property's salability if you choose to maintain large, old trees in it. Those mature trees are said to have a great impact on those who are looking into the land. In designing for your own landscape, remember the basic elements which are color, form, line, scale, and texture. Look at the project through an artist's eye.

Choose plants that look good when placed together or side by side in terms of their colors. Imagine what other people, especially the would-be buyer of the property, would feel upon seeing the colors that you chose for the project. Form is looking at the plants to be placed in the project in terms of their shape and branching patterns. Such factors should blend in with what one has planned for the whole landscape.

Line is according to the arrangement of the materials to be used in the design, how you plot them accordingly, as well as looking into their borders. Scale or the size of the plants that you want to use in the landscape design also determines the texture. The placing of each plant depending on its sizes would give one an idea about the texture because this factor is a visual matter.

Who Do You Like to Do It?

You could seek out professional help if you think that you cannot do it yourself. But with vast resources on landscape design, you might want to try browsing through them first and challenge yourself if you can do it before shelling out your money for someone else's services.

First, you need to observe other people's backyards. You might also want to ask how they have done it. Or if you see someone else doing such, all you have to do is watch the process and get inspiration from it. You can also find a wealth of information from landscaping books and magazines, television, and, of course, the Web.

Are You Up with the Plan?

Upon having the plan ready for your residential landscaping, you just have to ask yourself if you're up for it. Consider everything: the budget, the materials, your purpose for doing such, and the property itself, before plunging in and starting the process.

This book is also available in Kindle version

Made in the USA
Middletown, DE
31 October 2023

41709143R00070